Cancer: The Journey

Douglas R. Turner

May 10, 2019

Cancer: The Journey – Dedication

This paper is dedicated to any and all who have been stricken with cancer, often referred to as "The Emperor of All Maladies". It is also dedicated to their families, caregivers and to the medical community that exists to help those stricken to combat this dreadful disease.

It is also dedicated to my grandchildren, Charlotte Elizabeth Bunting and Ethan Hartman Gross, to thank them for the unconditional love and boundless joy they have brought into my life.

Cancer: The Journey – Introduction

Cancer is a very formidable disease. It takes many forms and has many stages. It is relentless, destructive, and seemingly has a "mind of its own", once it takes form within one's body. In this story, I will share my personal experience in confronting advanced stage metastatic prostate carcinoma in the hope that it may be helpful to anyone who learns they have cancer at some point in their life.

The book is organized into two sections. The first is a chronology starting from the very first indication I may have had prostate cancer through to today. The second section will present the many thoughts, perceptions, and adaptive processes I employed throughout the journey.

Section 1 – The Journey

In late August 2012, my primary care physician Dr. Steven Lieu expressed a concern to me during our post-physical exam discussion. "Doug", he said, "I'm very concerned about your prostate, especially the right-side lobe. My physical examination of it indicates it is very rigid and irregularly shaped, not soft and malleable as it should be. I think you should see a urologist as soon as possible and have a thorough examination of the prostate. Frankly, I'm very concerned about a possible malignancy. I'll give you a few names and please, act on this immediately."

My ride home was a bit of a blur. My immediate thoughts were less about me than how to break the news to my wife, Geri and my daughters, Sarah and Stephanie especially with Sarah scheduled to be married on September 7. After discussing the situation with Geri, I set about scheduling my urologist's appointment. Initially, in calling the group I was referred to, I was given an appointment for late October. That was fine with me, frankly, because I wanted to put it off anyway, using the wedding as a convenient excuse. It was your basic avoidance-avoidance move, classic denial on my part. As I had been asked to do, I called my primary care physician and relayed my scheduled appointment date. Shortly after that call, my phone rang. A very pleasant nurse advised me that two months was too long a period of time to wait. She would call the urology group on my behalf and see if a more immediate opening was available.

The next day Dr. Lieu's office called to say I had an appointment on Wednesday, September 5, 2012, thus two days before Sarah's wedding. This news initially did not please me. Now it would occur before the wedding leaving me with a potential dilemma. What should I tell my daughters, and when should I tell them? We decided to wait until after the appointment, and go forward depending upon what we learned. It was a bit of a juggling match, for sure.

My visit with the urologist, Dr. James Graydon, went well. One measurement the medical profession monitors as an indication of prostate problems is the prostate specific androgen (PSA) blood level. From my recent physical, the blood work had measured my PSA at approximately 2.72 ng/mL, well within the "normal" limits of 0-4.0 ng/mL. He was pleased with that result and we proceeded with the physical examination of the prostate. This exam is mildly intrusive but very necessary. Upon its completion, he declared that although the right lobe of my prostate was somewhat malformed, with a "ridge line" running across it and it also exhibited surface irregularities, which could be an indication of calcification, more commonly occurring as men age. But, he had seen such conditions before and was not overly concerned. I said, "Well, that's a relief. But, that said, Dr. Lieu had been very concerned about the physical attributes of the prostate and went so far as to refer to it as very likely to be a malignancy. It is quite an unexpected change in things to go from a week or so of thinking I may have prostate cancer to being told not to worry about it". "Doug", Dr. Graydon said, "this is what I do for a living. This is my specialty. Believe me, you're fine. We'll keep this on watch and stay out in front of it. I want you on a 90-day follow-up, blood work and physical exam. Before you leave, schedule a follow-up appointment for early December". As I was scheduling my next appointment, he came out into the waiting room and assured Geri all was well and we were good to go. With that in mind, I told both Sarah and Stephanie that evening what had transpired and that all was well, and we took off Thursday for Newport and Sarah and Jonathan's wedding weekend.

My December 2012 and March 2013 ninety-day follow-ups went well. PSA readings were stable at about 2.72 ng/mL and Dr. Graydon's examination of my prostate revealed no changes. So, he saw no need to see me in three months but rather scheduled me for a late September 2013 visit, now a six-month interval. It seemed to me we were going in the right direction, and it looked like I was coming out of the woods.

In early September 2013, I had my annual physical. Actually, I was hoping Dr. Lieu would skip my prostate exam since I was now on a six-month interval and was seeing Dr. Graydon later in the month (more avoidance). Dr. Lieu, however, never really shared the perspective of Dr. Graydon, but rather acquiesced to his perspective as the "expert" on the matter. Dr. Lieu advised we would proceed with the physical exam of the prostate because he wanted his own observations on the condition of the prostate, and whether anything had changed in the past year. The PSA blood level had elevated somewhat, up to 3.63 or so, but was still within "normal" levels. Regardless, he was concerned with the increase, which was about 30% in one interval. In the post-physical discussion, he spoke very frankly, once again, about his concern with his physical exam of the prostate. He asked me when I would next see Dr. Graydon, I told him my appointment was in about two weeks, scheduled for September 25. He implored of me to once again pass along his concerns and observations. I said that perhaps a phone call between the two would be helpful, I don't know if that ever occurred. What I do know is I was right back to square one, standing right where I'd been one year earlier. As Yogi might opine, it was "Déjà vu all over again". So, another long drive home and a revisit of the issue with my family.

On September 25, I again met with Dr. Graydon, who I had not seen since the previous March. As he entered the exam room, he said, "Doug, I don't like the PSA increase during this interval. Although it is still within "normal", it's about a 30+% jump, too much for six months." I said, "Well, since you mention it, I'd like to pass along Dr. Lieu's concern, as best I can impart it. I know you two have had different perspectives on the criticality of the physical condition of my prostate and what that may or may not indicate. But, he said to be sure you understood that I have two nodules extending from my right lobe, and significant surface irregularities and general hardness that concerns him greatly". "Let's have a look," Dr. Graydon said.

After a brief examination, he stepped back and said "Oh, things have changed considerably. It is quite different than your last check here in March. We are going to need a biopsy. We'll do that here, tomorrow". So, on September 26, I showed up for the biopsy. The biopsy was certainly one of the most unpleasant procedures I have ever endured. There is no direct access to the prostate, so the tissue samples are taken with a needle-like apparatus passing through the intestinal wall. Twelve samples are taken, six from each of the two lobes, right and left. So, there are twenty-four holes punched into your intestinal wall and prostate, which can take several weeks to heal. There are a few things to monitor, particularly the blood amount and color of it in the stool and/or urine and any possible indication of infection. I was told it would take seven to ten days to get the results, not counting Friday, September 27. Nothing to do but wait.

On Monday, October 7, my phone rang at mid-morning. The caller said Dr. Graydon would like to speak with me. I took that as not being a good sign, since with other tests in the past the "all clear" is typically given by a staff member. Sure enough, the word was that three of the twelve samples were positive, and it was confirmed I had prostate cancer. The next step was to come in for urological consultation. The game had changed, and not for the better.

Geri, Sarah, Stephanie and I met with Dr. Graydon the following Monday, October 14. We had a one-hour discussion of the biopsy results and possible action steps. Prostate biopsy samples are graded for malignancy on what is referred to as the Gleason scale. This is a combination of the grading of the sample by assigning a numeric value for the primary and secondary tumors on a scale of 0-5, with 5 being the most aggressive. The two values are then added for a total. The first number is most critical since it represents the primary tumor. For example, a Gleason rating of 4+3 =7 tumor tissue sample is of more concern than a 3+4=7 Gleason rating tissue sample, since the primary sample is more aggressive, having the higher-assigned value. The medical community considers a primary tumor rating of 4 or above and a total rating of 7 or above to be actionable. At least two of my samples were Gleason 4+3=7 so putting me "on watch" was not an option. A rating of 4+3=7 will, unattended, quickly become a rating of 5+3=8, or even 5+4 =9 as the secondary tumor grading will typically advance in like fashion. We were past "critical mass" so to speak, and had to develop a plan for curative intervention.

We began a discussion of alternative treatment options. Two viable forms of treatment, given my Gleason ratings, were either radiation of the prostate or surgery in the form of a radical prostatectomy. At that time, the biopsy indicted my cancer was

Stage IIA, meaning it was contained within the prostate and confined to one side of it. The surface of the prostate is a very thin-skinned layer of tissue, though, so it can be penetrated by the cancer somewhat easily as the cancer becomes more aggressive. After a thorough discussion of the "pros and cons" of each, I opted for the radical prostatectomy. All things considered, this seemed to provide the best overall chance for success, which I defined as eradication of the malignancy and extending my lifespan. It was time to take action.

I then called a urological oncologist, Dr. Anoop Meraney, recommended to me by Dr. Graydon, to schedule a consultation. Sarah was away on business, so Geri, Stephanie and I went to the appointment. We had an excellent discussion of the pending surgery and he briefed us thoroughly on the methodology for a radical prostatectomy, robotic surgery via the DaVinci robot, the protocols, and the projected recovery. Typically, a minimum of eight weeks is required between a prostate biopsy and prostate surgery because the biopsy itself is a form of surgery. So, with that in mind, surgery was scheduled for November 25, 2013. The point of no return had been reached, and I felt confident we were doing the right thing.

While waiting for my surgery, several tests were accomplished. Various CT scans were performed on my pelvis and abdomen and I also had a complete body bone scan. These scans were necessary because the medical approach is to treat the most advanced cancer first. So, if the scans had detected malignancy in my bones (principally the pelvis area), liver and/or lungs my prostatectomy would have been delayed until such malignancy was treated. Fortunately, all the scans came back negative, and the surgery stayed on schedule. However, as there is so many times with cancer, there was a bit of a qualifier tucked in. Even the most sophisticated scanning equipment cannot detect an irregularity (cancer) unless the particle is at least the size of a pencil point. So, while we were not 100% sure I had no remote site malignancy, by every acceptable medical protocol there was no reason to not proceed with my scheduled surgery.

My surgery, performed by Dr. Meraney, took place on November 25, 2013, but was not without an issue or two. What should have been about a 2 ½ to 3-hour procedure took 6 1/2 hours. Much of the additional time was dedicated to carefully detaching the right lobe of my prostate from the nerve system of the rectum. It had to be peeled from the rectal wall prior to being removed. I am very grateful to Dr. Meraney for his skill and patience on this matter. A less successful extraction of the prostate could have resulted in a colostomy. Thankfully, that was avoided, and the surgery was a success. After a two-day stay, I came home from the hospital the day before Thanksgiving. The next ten days were spent extending my best efforts to be "up and about" as much as possible, hindered somewhat by the presence of the catheter and the drainage apparatus for the removal of post-op body fluids. One responsibility I had was to carefully observe and measure the daily amount of bodily fluid discharged, since it was important to have this amount lessen to the point of cessation by the end of day ten. Fortunately, it decreased daily, slowly at first and then at an accelerated rate.

In early December, I had a follow-up appointment with Dr. Meraney to remove both the catheter and body fluid drain receptacles and to discuss with him the post-op pathology. The initial part of the appointment consisted of removing the bodily fluid discharge drain receptacles and then injecting 270 ml of saline solution into my bladder through the catheter. At that point, the catheter was removed, and I was given a few minutes to excrete that exact amount of solution into a container. Fortunately, I was able to do this, so my catheter was removed. The second requirement for urination was that I had to urinate normally within six hours after leaving the office. Should I not be able to, I was instructed that I must then return to the hospital emergency room for reinsertion of the catheter. One issue many men encounter after a radical prostatectomy is regaining continence. Many, up to 30%, end up having to return to the catheter on a permanent basis. I was determined to have that not occur in my case.

After I completed the nurse's phase of the appointment, Dr. Meraney came in to discuss the post-op pathology report. At first glance, I felt the news might not be encouraging, and it wasn't. As part of the surgical protocol for the radical prostatectomy he took five lymph nodes from the surrounding area, three from the right side, and two from the left. The pathology indicted that one of the left side nodes was malignant, and graded as Stage IV carcinoma. So, what I thought would be a day of getting rid of all the post-surgical trappings and going home to continue my recuperation became something else quite beyond that. This was definitely not a turn for the better. I did get one small victory in that I was able to urinate on my own within the six hours, and escaped further use of the catheter. Although I was told I would have to wear an adult diaper for the next few months that was a small price to pay for removal of the catheter. One item of note: Because the right side of the prostate was significantly worse in structure and appearance, Dr. Meraney initially felt that if the cancer had passed into the lymph system it would have been in the right-side nodes. Yet, according to the pathology, it actually was found on the left. Had he not taken lymph nodes from both sides, although the left side appeared "clean", he would have missed the cancer in my system.

One silver lining in the cloud is that prostate cancer metastasizes at a slower rate than other malignancies. The preferred medical approach is to wait as long as possible after the radical prostatectomy before starting additional requisite treatment, should any be necessary. Data has shown that there is no benefit, in terms of survivability, to starting treatment shortly after surgery. There is, however, a potential downside, particularly with radiation treatment, if the surgical wounds have not completely healed. There can be significant damage to the tissues including the possible introduction of a future malignancy from the radiation. With such a large potential downside, and no apparent upside, the longer one can wait, the better the chances for a successful outcome So, I was scheduled for a two-step 30 and 90-day blood test. If the 30-day test measured PSA below 0.10 ng/mL, I could go the next interval, thus to 90 days for the 2nd blood test. That would be the "best case" scenario, giving my body the preferred interval for healing prior to commencing with the radiation.

The thirty days seemed an eternity, passing at a snail's pace. The first results were much better than expected, registering well below the required "less than 0.1ng/mL.". My surgeon was very pleased with this and felt we could go to the full 90-day interval with no issues. This 30-day test is very important. Had my PSA blood level been greater than 0.1ng/mL, treatment would need to be initiated immediately, and the potential damage to unhealed tissue would be deemed an acceptable risk under the circumstances. So, one bullet dodged. The

90-day interval came in early March, 2014 and corresponded with a doctor's visit to discuss both the results and the upcoming treatment composition and schedule. Once again, my PSA blood level was well below the "less than 0.1ng/mL". Dr. Meraney decided, based on this, that there was still time to let the surgical healing continue and indicated my treatment would begin in early May. The protocol would consist of thirty-six treatments of radiation combined with hormone therapy. The hormone therapy would start in April, three or four weeks before the radiation. The hormone therapy is based on the concept of androgen deprivation, administered in the form of injections of Lupron, an artificial hormone that blocks the body's creation of testosterone, which is the major source of energy necessary for the prostate carcinoma to further metastasize. Denied the necessary androgen by the blocking of testosterone, the prostate carcinoma cells become very lethargic, even static, and go into a state of suspension, making them "easy targets" for the radiation beams. The radiation beams, when applied, break down the DNA structure of the malignant cells and destroy them. So, the hormone treatments and radiation serve as a very effective "one-two" punch against the malignancy.

My radiation treatments were administered from May to June, 2014. About a week before the radiation sessions began, I had a pre-treatment doctor's visit with my radiological oncologist, Dr. Timothy Boyd, and various technicians. This visit consisted of getting a baseline CT scan of my abdomen, being fitted for a lower-body molding, receiving very clear dietary guidelines for the treatment period and meeting with Dr. Boyd to discuss my upcoming treatments. These treatments would occur daily, Monday-Friday, for seven plus weeks. The baseline CT scan of my abdomen was necessary to determine the three access points for the upcoming radiation, which was targeted for my prostate cavity and surrounding lymph areas. Once these access points were mapped, I was marked with three small "tattoos", one on each side of my hips and one below the navel. This was done in concert with forming the body molding. For each treatment, I would be placed in the same position via the body molding, and the radiation beams would be aligned with each of the tattoos. This approach assured I would always get the radiation delivered to the correct internal sites. For the radiation to be successful and to minimize collateral damage to surrounding organs and tissues, a strict dietary regime is necessary. Anything that would bloat the gas path and/or produce gas must be eliminated from one's diet during the treatment period. Most fresh fruits and raw vegetables (as well as many cooked ones), many fried foods, dairy, red meats, fiber, carbonated beverages, and alcohol are thus eliminated from the daily diet. A very bland diet of white bread, fish, rice cakes, peanut butter, tea, saltines, eggs and other foodstuffs that do not promote bloating of the gas path is requisite. The mantra for radiation treatment for the abdominal area is "empty bowel, full bladder". An empty bowel collapses out of the way of the radiation on its path to the target areas, and a full bladder floats up out of the path of the same radiation beams. Ensuring the bladder was full was pretty easy, I just drank 24 to 30 ounces of water about 30 minutes before my scheduled radiation. The empty bowel took some coordinating. I selected 11:45 as my daily appointment time with that in mind. Once I adjusted to my new diet, it went quite smoothly.

The machine used for my radiation treatments was a Varian Trilogy linear accelerator. This is a very sophisticated machine that enables the radiation to be administered very accurately to the target areas. As radiation can destroy both healthy and malignant cells, it is critical that the radiation beams be delivered to the target areas as precisely as possible. While I was held in place by the body molding, the table upon which I was placed was shifted into position, and the machine was readied for application. The technicians ensure that everything is in alignment and then the radiation is administered. The actual treatment time was about fifteen minutes per daily dosage. Much of the time was spent with the machine positioning itself for the next radiation dosage. The actual radiation time is a matter of a few seconds.

Each Tuesday during my treatment interval, I met with Dr. Boyd. He reviewed my treatment data and images stored in his laptop with me and answered any questions I may have had. It was basically a "here's where we are, and where we're going" update. When my treatment was completed, he scheduled me for a thirty-day follow-up, including blood work, for late July. My PSA blood level actually increased slightly during the period of my treatment, to 0.02 ng/mL. This, however, was not of concern to my doctors, since it was well below the level that would indicate a potential issue, that being 0.10 ng/mL. He then scheduled me for a six-month follow-up appointment in late January 2015.

The next step would be receiving my second Lupron injection from Dr. Meraney's nurse in early October. I had more blood work in late September and the PSA blood level was back to "less than" 0.02 ng/mL once again. The second injection of Lupron is required to ensure that any potentially remaining cancer cells do not metastasize until the effects of the radiation have completely destroyed them (should they not be already). It seemed to me to be a kind of insurance injection, given "just-in-case". A six-month follow-up appointment was then scheduled with Dr. Meraney, as the Lupron injections were administered by his office. The appointment was set for early April, 2015, to coincide with the Lupron shot wearing off, as it is effective for six months.

My January and April 2015 visits were uneventful. The blood work was once again excellent and both Dr. Boyd and Dr. Meraney were very pleased. Dr. Boyd said it was no longer necessary for me to see him regularly, and referred my ongoing treatment back to Dr. Meraney. I received my third Lupron injection during the April visit and pressed on. I accepted the fact that the Lupron was required to ensure any remaining cancer in my system did not further metastasize. Lupron, as I indicated earlier, by shutting down the body's production of testosterone through the process of androgen deprivation, acts to combat the spread of the cancer from the lymph system to any other areas, the bones, lungs, and liver being primary targets for metastatic prostate carcinoma. That said, the Lupron also completely robbed me of all my stamina, strength, endurance and, starting my second year of it was a bit daunting. Frankly, I was in a chronic state of 24/7 exhaustion.

My October 2015 oncology visit with Dr. Meraney also went very well. The blood work was excellent, and the cancer seemed well under control. But, at this visit, I had my first point of contention with Dr. Meraney. I was due for another Lupron shot. The protocol for someone with advanced stage metastatic carcinoma was six injections over three years. I was halfway through. But, I did not want another injection. I told him as such, no more Lupron. He did not agree. After a frank and focused discussion, we reached an agreement. Because my PSA blood count was so low, less than 0.02ng/mL (within the margin of accuracy of the instrument's ability to measure), we agreed that I could forego the injection but would need a blood test at 90 days. The slightest increase in my PSA level, any movement towards 0.1ng/mL, back on the Lupron I would be. For the next twelve months, with four blood draws, there was no increase, none whatsoever. Dr. Meraney was very pleased and as he phrased it, "pleasantly surprised". By this time, much of my body strength had recovered and with it, my overall outlook.

Things went along on course until the fall of 2017. One evening, with no prior warning or indication of a problem, I had a considerable amount of blood in my urine. This, I must say, was somewhat alarming and unsettling. I had not had such an occurrence of this since my initial prostate biopsy in 2013, which had been expected. A day or two went by, and I had a second occurrence, this time with much darker blood and much more of it. I actually thought I might bleed out, and, found myself getting lightheaded. It finally stopped, but being the second such occurrence in two days, I next called Dr. Meraney.

Because blood in the urine is a rather serious matter, Dr. Meraney saw me promptly and performed a cystoscopy, a rather unpleasant procedure whereby a camera is inserted into the urethra and then pushed up through the urethra into the bladder, thought to be the source of the blood in the urine. The camera photos confirmed this as radiation-induced cystitis was visible on the surface of the bladder with a considerable amount was also found around the mouth of the bladder. The specific bleeding condition is referred to as hematuria, confirmed by Dr. Meraney as being caused by the radiation therapy in 2014. This condition occurs in about 18% of cases like mine, and the median occurrence interval is 35 months from exposure to the radiation beams, mine being 37 months. I have to say I was a bit taken aback by the damage to the bladder. Much was made of all the precautions taken in preparing for my radiation treatment from the body cast to the accuracy of the beam(s) to the "full bladder" mantra. As well, each day I had implored of the technicians to not activate the beams until they had perfect three-dimensional alignment. We were where we were however, the damage was irreversible, and my bladder was now on the watch list. An additional concern, of course, was that the damaged bladder tissue could, at some point, become cancerous itself. I had just about achieved a sort of stases on the whole cancer situation, but this was, undeniably, a new issue to be on watch for. I scheduled a follow-up cystoscopy for my next visit, and headed for home. I had a few more occurrences of blood in my urine before my next cystoscopy, which was to be expected, but they were less severe than my earlier ones, with more time in between.

My second cystoscopy showed that there was no additional radiation damage evident. We had discussed taking a tissue biopsy from some of the affected areas but Dr. Meraney felt the tissue did not appear to be cancerous. So, he deferred on the biopsy pending any further incidences of blood in the urine. From this visit until my next scheduled visit in April 2018 there were no further incidences of bleeding, nor were there any during the interval between then and my next visit in November 2018. My blood work was also excellent during this time period. This was very encouraging and quite a relief. My November 2018 visit was a landmark visit in that I was placed on a one-year appointment interval, with blood work due at six months. So, in May of 2019, my PSA will be checked, but, by now, I see that as a routine precaution.

Cancer: The Journey Section II

Being advised one has advanced stage metastatic carcinoma is, without a doubt, a life-changing event. This section of the book will present my thinking, rationale, and actions taken from the very beginning of the journey up to today.

1.   Initial Thoughts and Decisions

When I first learned of my cancer from the results of my initial prostate biopsy, my focus was on survivability. What did I have to do to give myself the best opportunity for long-term survivability? I've long been a fan of Steven Covey, so I took one of his Seven Habits, "Begin with the end in mind" as my mantra. The end of all this for me was to survive the ordeal and restore as much of my health and well-being as possible. I thought two factors were critical. Firstly, was that one of my four doctors must be the primary owner of my situation and care. Four was too many, and I did not want to have to run everything by four doctors to try to gain consensus. Once I opted for surgery, I decided that Dr. Meraney was my best choice and he graciously accepted my asking that role of him. So, he and I would agree on all actions going forward, and the others would be advised as Dr. Meraney saw appropriate. This turned out to be fortuitous because, when my post-operative pathology indicated the carcinoma in my lymph system, Dr. Meraney, also being my surgeon, was best positioned to be going forward with me. The second factor was complete agreement with Dr. Meraney on what the end goal of the journey was. I wanted to take whatever action, surgical, post-surgical, and ongoing that gave me the best opportunity to survive, heal, and restore myself to a quality of life close to what I enjoyed when we started. That became our definition of success. Everything we decided, from then on, was against that backdrop. We were "Beginning with the end in mind", and agreed on what that was to be.

I also had my own personal view on my illness. I saw cancer as an offensive invader, a disruptor, a sneaky, devious, scheming antagonist that was out to destroy me. Simply put, I would either eradicate the cancer, or it would me. I was not going to "learn to live with it" or redefine myself around it. I would dispense with it, and go on with my life, or have no life. So, armed with that resolve, I engaged the enemy.

2.   Taking Inventory

As I was orienting myself to what lay ahead, I looked around at what I had to work with and how I could best use such assets to achieve my goal of survivability coupled with restoration of health and general well-being. I will share some of this inventory now as an example of the technique I employed. I was sixty-seven years old when I learned of the severity of the cancer. I had retired from my place of employment and thus had no job to maintain during my illness. This is a big responsibility to be relieved of. It gave me complete freedom of schedule and treatment without the concern of how that would impact my employment. My daughters were both grown, well-educated professionals, married and well-positioned to go on without me, if it came to that. Their daily lives and fundamental well-being were not at risk. Our house was long since paid off, so we had no mortgage worries. I was in overall excellent health. My weight was well within due bounds, no issues with cholesterol, no diabetes, no high blood pressure, no medications, and no other form of illness. As Dr. Lieu said, "You are in excellent overall shape, except for the cancer". I thought about that when he said it, and burst out laughing. I told him I knew how he meant it, and that he was not making light of things. But, it caught my fancy anyway and gave me a good chuckle. Dr. Meraney also cited my overall health and said he could develop a very aggressive treatment protocol and was confident my body could tolerate it. By the time I finished taking this inventory of what assets I had at my disposal, actually writing everything down and examining each, I felt very confident I was well-positioned to successfully achieve my goal. This was a very valuable endeavor and one I harkened back to many times over the next few years. I redefined it a bit to "take the positive inventory" because, each time I honestly reviewed what I had going for myself, I felt more positive about my chances.

3.   Knowledge

While I was recovering from my surgery and awaiting the upcoming treatment which would ensue, I decided I would set out to learn as much as I could about the disease I now had. My decision was driven by a desire to increase my understanding, so I could better communicate with Dr. Meraney, and later, with my radiologist, Dr. Boyd, who worked closely with Dr. Meraney. My thinking on this aspect of my treatment was it would make my doctor's visits much more productive, and my treatment regimen that much more effective. With Dr. Meraney's guidance, I selected credible, legitimate, recognized sources like Memorial Sloan Kettering, Dana Farber, Mayo Clinic, Johns Hopkins, the Prostate Cancer Foundation, and the American Cancer Society. Also, I want to mention Dr. David Samadi, who I became aware of from the television show House Calls. Like Dr. Meraney, Dr. Samadi is a recognized leader in the field of prostate cancer surgery and treatment, both being early pioneers in utilizing the DaVinci robotic technique. Beyond House Calls, I follow Dr. Samadi on Facebook, and his knowledge of prostate cancer and its ongoing treatment accelerated my learning process immeasurably. I read much of the material online, but made copies of what I thought to be the most significant articles. I built several notebooks that way, organized by topic, updated as necessary.

Perhaps the most significant benefit from my effort to educate myself on the cancer occurred quite unexpectedly and in the form of a very subtle transformation. I became very interested in my cancer and cancer in general. Learning about it became my raison d'être, and at some point, I realized I had taken all the mystery out of it, eliminated the unknowns, supplanted unknowns with knows, replaced fear of the unknown with knowledge and gained increasing confidence that we were out in front of this disease. We had taken the upper ground, we were on the offensive, and we now had cancer on the run and would prevail. Cancer no longer had any hold on me. I am not overstating this, I offer it in complete sincerity because it is exactly what transpired.

4.   Exercise

The last thing you want to do when you're exhausted is exercise. That seems pretty self-evident. When you have cancer, and when you are in treatment for it, exhaustion is quite common, so it takes great commitment to exercise in any form. But, the medical community stresses the importance of exercise as an important contributor to recovery. I elected to walk, and walk, and walk. Inside, outside, up and down stairways, it didn't matter. When I started the program in 2014, Fitbit was not yet available, so I tried to walk for one hour each day. I used a time factor rather than a distance because it was easy to break into increments and I was not concerned with pace. I am now into my 6th year of walking, and armed with my Fitbit Charge 3 have my daily step total, distance walked, and time spent exercising measured with precision. My favorite place for walking has become along the CT River at the Glastonbury Boathouse.

5.   Diet and Nutrition

I had long since forsworn alcohol and tobacco, so there were two key health items that needed no addressing. Once I had completed my radiation treatments, during which a very specific diet had to be followed, I opted for a diet very close to the Mediterranean diet, with chicken, fish, vegetables and fruits being the basic components. I also incorporated three somewhat unique additions, two of my own making, one from a study published by Dr. Samadi. The first one is an elixir I make and consume daily which consists of one rounded teaspoon of ground ginger root, one rounded teaspoon of ground turmeric root, black pepper (to increase the digestion effectiveness of the turmeric) and two tablespoons of 100% virgin olive oil, first cold press (the top-rated for purity California Olive Ranch brand). Ginger and turmeric both provide anti-inflammatory benefits and some clinical trials have shown them to be effective agents against certain forms of metastatic cancers. Secondly, I eat four cloves of raw garlic daily. Beyond being an anti-bacterial compound, garlic is thought to be effective in combating certain forms of metastatic cancer. I eat the cloves raw, because the benefit of garlic falls off significantly if the garlic is heated above 140 degrees F. Lastly is a mixture of "tree nuts" comprised of pistachios, walnuts, pecans and almonds. Dr., Samadi published the results of a Swedish study of select groups of men who had prostate cancer treatment and the group who ate the "tree nuts" had significantly extended life spans. While it is difficult to say precisely why the "tree nuts" were effective, the results of the study seemed to validate the benefit to the participants who consumed them. I also eliminated the use of refined sugar because it is thought to be a potential energy source for any post-treatment remaining cancer cells. I also do not use any artificial sweeteners. Instead, I use a natural no-calorie sweetener, Stevia.

6.   Perspective and Outlook

My approach from the start was to treat my cancer journey as a learning experience (albeit a form of "crash course"). I measured everything against a "can't hurt, might help" metric. The dietary and exercise regimens fell into that category. I returned to reading extensively, not just about cancer, but many forms of fiction and non-fiction by authors and in areas of interest to me. I also listened to music, sometimes just on the main player but also with my headphones later in the evening. I also continued watching the NY Yankees on YES with Michael Kay and his crew.

One aspect of my treatment that impacted me greatly was my daily treatment at the Helen and Harry Gray Cancer Center - Hartford Health Care. Sitting in the atrium waiting to be called into the waiting room area, I witnessed people of all ages and from all walks of life. All were there for cancer treatment, either infusion (chemotherapy) or radiation, or both. After a week or so, one begins to recognize quite a few folks as appointment times tend to be consistent, once treatment starts. This is especially true when you sit in the inner waiting room in the specific treatment area.

While waiting, some patients seemed to want to talk about their illness, others did not. Most were accompanied by a sibling, or friend, or parent, or grown child. I had no sense, prior to this, for how many lives are adversely impacted by this disease, and the time, effort and expense associated with cancer treatment. Above and beyond this is the stress, anxiety and resultant emotional wear and tear not just on the patient but also on all the good people providing support and being an active part of the treatment effort, whatever the outcome. While recognizing that every patient was potentially gravely ill, there were some occasions I witnessed where it was abundantly clear what the outcome would inevitably be. Those situations were particularly heart-rending. Five years later, I carry these images with me, as, I expect, would anyone who underwent a similar experience.

Another decision I made was I would fiercely maintain my capacities and independence as long as I possibly could, surrendering any ability to be self-sufficient only begrudgingly. I'll share two examples. Although some good folks offered to drive me to Hartford for treatment, I declined their generosity and drove myself to and from each treatment session. To me, any form of accepting help represented a step towards relinquishing my independence. A second example is a bit more personal, but represents the same point equally well. I would need to wear an "adult diaper" for an indefinite period of time. The surgery, despite the precision made possible with a skilled surgeon and a DaVinci robot, of necessity requires the removal of a section of the urethra because it passes through the prostate gland which is removed in its entirety. There can also be some nerve impairment and other aftereffects which contribute to many men having difficulty with incontinence post-surgery, thus the diaper. In many cases, the incontinence is permanent. Thinking back, I wore these diapers for a few days, and then stopped. I simply refused to wear a diaper and I haven't since. It should be noted that I had, and have, no issue with continence. Again, I saw that as another slip into dependency (no pun intended with Depends) and a loss in my capability and independence. Grown men do not wet their pants, it's that simple.

7.   Support Group

My support group was quite informal and very unstructured, but it was an effective one, regardless. As word got out about my cancer diagnosis, different people reached out via email, a phone call, a card in the mail, or through a family member. Although I had not been active in the Marlborough Congregational Church for many years, Pastor Bob, the Care Team, and many other good folks expressed their concern, wished me well, offered their help, and kept me in their prayers. My immediate family served as a Board of Directors of sorts, and was actively involved each step of the way. I was deeply touched that people who had their own issues and problems to deal with on a daily basis would take the time to think of me and reach out. Several of my old workmates from P&W stayed in regular contact with me to the point that I would write them email summaries of each of my doctor's visits, test results, decisions, etc., and this practice continued for a few years until my condition became less guarded and it looked like I was getting into the clear. My interface with all the people who reached out was guided by my earlier-explained thoughts on maintaining my independence. I simply did not want to slip into a pattern of dependency. So, while I was always grateful for their outreach, I always politely declined any offer of help. I took ownership of my own situation, and prime responsibility for its outcome.

8.   Faith

This is a subject I want to include, as a reminder to the reader to draw upon their faith, whatever that may be, as they see fit. It is a very personal matter, and beyond my reach to suggest anything beyond that. Let it be a source of strength as you confront the illness just as you use your faith in all other aspects of your daily life. "To thine own self be true" fits nicely here.

9.   Survivor's Guilt

I had heard of this phenomenon before when reading about tragic accidents, military operations, school shootings and other events where death occurs and someone in the midst of it all somehow escapes relatively intact. I was not prepared, however, as it related to cancer. From the time I took ill until today, five very good friends of mine were stricken by, and died from cancer. Also, a grandson of a friend of mine died from cancer, as did a schoolmate of my granddaughter. So, here I am pressing on towards my goal of surviving and no less than seven people I was associated with had died, six of them being stricken well after I had been. The emotions one feels in this situation are very complex and difficult to articulate. In simplest form, they can be expressed as "Why me? Why am I still alive and they are not?" This thought nagged at me for several months. To get beyond it, I finally encapsulated it into one simple thought. "Grace, like rain, falls on the just and the unjust". And so, I reasoned, does cancer. It strikes anyone at its own will, and in its own time. Cancer does not play favorites and does not pick victims. Some people survive the ordeal and some (many, perhaps most) do not. They say you cannot put the genie back into the bottle. That may be true. But, you'd better find a way to deal with this issue should it present itself because you cannot spend the remainder of your life which you fought so hard to preserve feeling guilty that you lived, and others did not.

Douglas R. Turner is a retiree, having completed a tour of duty in the United States Air Force and a successful career in aerospace. In his mid-late 60s, he was stricken with advanced stage prostate carcinoma in his lymph system. Today, based upon the most recent testing evidence, he is cancer-free.

This book is a chronicle of his medical path to recovery and ultimate healing. It provides concise, insightful step-by-step explanations of why he and his medical team made the decisions they did, and the contributions these decisions made towards the successful outcome of their effort. Although written specifically for patients with prostate cancer, this book is intended to be of help to anyone learning they have cancer of any type.